The Dance of Life

The Dance of Life

India Russell

Godstow Press

First published 2010 by
Godstow Press
60 Godstow Road
Wolvercote
Oxford OX2 8NY
www.godstowpress.co.uk

ISBN 978-1-907651-01-4

The publishers are grateful to Stacey International for their kind
permission to reproduce 'The Secret High Jumper' from India
Russell's 'The Kaleidoscope of Time'.

Typeset in Centaur by Jean Desebrock of Alacrity
Cover design by Linda Proud

Printed and bound by Imprint Academic, Exeter, Devon

CONTENTS

Final Notes to a Dancer

This, then, is the space in which to choreograph your life.
Note the overarching trees, gnarled trunks
Perfect proscenium for the action you'll invent.
Admire the pale-washed cyclorama with slowly moving
                                      rose-pink clouds
Forming the familiar everchanging backdrop. Although,
                        we have to warn you,
Occasionally, strange, ancient machinery, forgotten in the flies,
Grinds, ghostlike, into action, releasing filthy plumes of dust
Turning the clouds to ominous precursors of Jove's ire.

Beware of this. Beware, also, dim
Shifting areas, upstage left and right –
Sulking, sucking bogs refusing to be fenced.
Even the Danger signs have been
Drawn down into their deathly depths.

Tread carefully. Particularly when you meet
Those crushing humans, eyes lustingly fixed upon
The spotlight. Avoid such contacts. But
Don't forget to dance. Dance and weave new patterns
With all life just waiting in the wings.

Dance in secret shapes of brilliance
Dance and give the pulsing world your breathtaking design –
Oh, dance, before the *deus ex machina*
Descends and takes you to another stage
Beyond this known proscenium, bright spotlight
                     and beguiling cyclorama.

Feet Off Ground

Strange places we designated
As exempt from being caught –
Walls, hillocks are understandable
Even drain covers; but faint crosses
In the ground,
Lightenings in the grass, the curve of a
Lane or road – but only one
Particular place, known by us
But to the uninitiated eye
Undiscernible – a large leaf,
A twig, a shadow even, were refuges from 'It',
A breathing space in which to rest, gain strength
Then plunge into the game,
Although I can't remember the continuing race
Only the feeling of utter safety
Despite the fact one was not hidden
Was there before the enemy,
Heart racing, terror gradually subsiding,
Yet inviolable.

And suddenly, today, feeling pursued,
By what? It? My own particular Fate?,
I saw our childish sanctuaries again,
Felt again the outpouring relief of Home
And wished it were so simple, now, to
Designate a leaf, a turning in the road,
                    to be my Feet Off Ground.

The Return

She was a schoolgirl again in her dream
And frightened of the curving path that
Was always there, waiting for her.
The two boys she was laughing with
Offered to accompany her but she
Was still apprehensive of
The horrible, lurking place she'd have to pass
And the ever-hostile curve.

She was safe with them
Feeling her tremulous femininity surrounded
By their burgeoning maleness - it was
Familiar and warm; but the dark path led
Into the threatening unknown
And she was loth to venture on it.

Night passed and
As the path dissolved, the sleeper stirred.
Quickly her soul re-entered
Through her open back
And the busy molecules
Reshaped her into daily human form,
Pulling her reluctantly awake
As she watched the silent streamers of
Reality
        dissolve upon the day.

The Secret High Jumper

After school, on the hushed, summer-warm playing field,
No one at the classroom windows but the occasional
Lone girl, kept in on detention,
I would practise, or rather, exult in,
High Jump.

The run-up, the sudden lift-off from familiar grass
Into the ever-changing, school-free air
Which slowly and securely embraced my sailing body
Was quite magical. If I'd grown wings
I could not have felt more earth-free or released.

And then the gentle landing, seemingly hours after,
When I would quietly, as though not wishing to disturb
Propitious gods, raise the bar
Run back to my soft starting place
And once again begin my wonderful ascent. It was
Intoxicating. God-given. And a Secret.

But then, one day, the striding Games Mistress just happened
To see me. I, who was 'unsporty', 'bright', 'silly'
'Boy-mad' (and, for some reason, a school prefect)
Was now to Represent The School.
And at the first bleak Competition, my god of flight
Deserted me. There, on that loud Athletics Ground
Where tough-limbed, strutting girls in masterful shorts and spikes

Measured professional paces to the bar
I, who'd never counted but just jumped,
Became uncertain, wavered, copied their proud movements
And was, of course, disqualified.
'Three No-Jumps!' rang across my heat-hazed head.
And grounded in the adult, grey-dimensional world
                              I took the sad bus home.

And often in this heavy time
I suddenly glimpse those far-off, sunny days
And wish, oh wish
I'd never doubted
            I could fly.

The Forbidden Garden

It was the longed-for final day at school.
At last, I was to enter that forbidden greeny glade
     the out-of-bounds Elysium
Temptingly glimpsed through all the regimented toils of years.

The little gate was magically unlocked
And, no lessons ever again, no reprimands,
No homework, no tedious assemblies,
No examinations, no reports,
We three prefects entered in upon the
First stage of our freedom, the first stage of
Our journey into that so often talked-of state of adulthood.

We stood, at first, the gate behind us now,
Entranced by the embracing greenness, and then,
Remembering our daring plan, we stripped off
Our dull uniforms, our lace-up shoes and socks,
Revealing bright bikinis and white, tender forms,
Butterflies or fairies emerging from a pupa,
And we danced and danced
The bushes dancing with us, birds singing a refrain,
The leaves and trees all humming and the
Freeing air caressing our young bodies,
Lorraine and Ronnie and myself.

It was a dance of innocent and youthful joy, but it was
As well, a dance of sad farewell
For when, uniformed again, we went and said goodbye
To all the teachers, and our form mistress,
       I wept.

The Castle

I was there, within the castle walls
Dancing with the 'chinless wonders', as we flippantly called them,
Wondering at the tattered banners pendant in the ballroom,
The great log fires flickering in the halls.

Wondering at a thrilling life dictated by its power
A life of elegant subservience to its sway,
The balls and parties, deferential servants
And, oh glory, the perfect garments tended by one's maid.

Nearly, so very nearly, I was caught in it,
Rescued by a Knight from everyday,
Protected from the horrible hurly-burly
The simple light of common people gay.

Nearly, so very nearly, I was to glitter
At balls, grand dinners, and by day,
Elegant and smiling;
And in fee.
In fee to the great family traditions
Their tedious tales of ancient battles grey
Fought to gain the Castle and the drawbridge
Pulled up against the rascals and the day.

In fee to history's coloured stories of our conquerors
The gallant heroes who kept this Island free,
Protected her from awful heathen bounders
And made us masters of the glittering sea.

Their banners then hung high above the ballroom –
Strange, bloody decorations for we innocent young
Dancing with the charming chinless wonders
Whose daring exploits were, as yet, unsung.

And sometimes at the stony casement window
I recognise my youthful, lonely self
Leaning on the unforgiving stonework
And gazing sadly at the distant beckoning day.

Vision

Never dreaming in my dream
That they'd be there
I turned and saw the mountains.

I'd climbed alone
Up to pure rolling heights, amazed to find
New sparkling landscapes of the mind
When, turning at the distant sound of thunder,
I suddenly saw them –

First one, then two and then a vista,
Bright mountains rising in the
                      hazy, distant air.
A joyful recognition pulsed through every vein,
This then was why I'd climbed, unknowing,
                  to such heights.

Relieved, as though a heavy veil had been discarded,
I traced again my musing pathway down
But entering bounden time
I found I'd left it all too late to
Travel up to London to the lecture.

I tried to telephone to ascertain its length
                – perhaps to hear the second half
Would be acceptable?
But now the thunderstorm was overwhelming
Crashing round the house
Sparks leaping out of power points and lights.

    And so I waited, thinking of the mountains

And then a most familiar but completely unknown man
          came in and joined me and we sat
          in that storm-circled house
          in warm companionship
          life springing in my very centre
          from the vision and
          his welcome radiance;

We grew towards embrace but then my former lover crashed in
          thunderous like the weather,
          slammed some books and papers on a shelf
                              and left.
     And suddenly I was alone again, deserted.

     But still those mountains towered in my mind,
     Another world – a world that I could enter if I chose.
     The thunder ceased and then a voice said clearly,
          You need to be alone
               to see the mountains.

The Silent Shores

A long journey it is, to the
Land of Dreams;
Down through shores of silence.
First the black beach and the
Unpredictable sea, then falling
Further to the next and next
And nothing but the stones and vastness
Of the night and all the time the
Continual movement down and down
Through countless shores. All slightly
Different – all seemingly deserted
But for your warm, helpless self
Falling wonderingly through them;
Until you meet your dreams
                and are free of Time's pathetic grasp.

But then, your visionary visit over,
The sad and difficult return – the
Awkward stages pulling
You up and up, through those same shores but
Travelling now through fast evolving years,
From childhood through each changing phase
Until you surface into Earthly time-bound being and
Noisy day shakes you awake into
The glaring and impossible world.

The Dance of Mysteries

Pulsing from a distant star,
Or was it from the balmy groves of Plato,
The secret, heavenly music
Sang out
Lifting her into a dance
Of supernatural design.

    With speed of rushing wind,
    Her draperies flowing after her,
    She shaped the entrancing air
    With Grecian forms of elemental force;

    She turned and flew and then, like
    Crashing, green-lit waves,
    Fell, dispersed and seemed to disappear
    Until the divine rhythms drew her back
    Into the pulse and whirl of the
    Compelling dance, which further traced
    Strange shapes and angles, flashing turns
    And leaps, casting bright shadows
    On the listening stars
    Returning their music with delighted, loving thanks;

Then, gradually, she awoke
Into the grey and puzzling day;
The divinely-patterned dance
Retreated into mystery
And she was left alone, exhausted,
But secure in its reality.

Half waking at the moon's first glance

At the moon's first glance
I remember my ballet shoes.
He has been unfaithful again
In my dreams.
Shall I draw him back
With my dancing?

Seismograph

The reverberations of experience
Surge through my body, shifting
My very core
So I am not
What I was before.

A baffled, beautiful young horse
Glimpsed in a concrete jail
Makes me shape Pegasus wings
To help us fly beyond all mortal things.

I want to gallop, rushing through the wind
But cannot stand or fly the glaring, human day
                              that stones our bodies

And I am lost as he
In outraged, lonely agony.

Vibrations

I know how you felt, my family, my family,
Antennae constantly alert
Registering, unwillingly, the terrible vibrations
Of the world

Never finding rest but only further
Confirmation of the awful chaos and
The gleaming symmetry of creation
In the microcosmic works of scientists
And artists. But Bach and Schubert
Cannot help and nor can Schrödinger,
Except for that one passage where you, my
Father, always wept.

And now I weep unceasingly
As your vibrations – oh, my mother and my father
And oh, my long-missed brother –
Sing within me
                while, without, the
Terrible world rains down its horror
                        and its unbelief.

Black and Blue
to Nina Simone

Dear Nina
America also cast out Isadora
Cast her out for dancing Truth and Freedom,
          two words the hypocrites can't bear.
But like yours, her spirit was beyond the reach of colourless and petty men
          grounded in their smugly fenced-in worlds,
Crossing continents and barriers with its fire.

She talked to Russian Communists with no knowledge of the language
Charmed Stanislavsky, while the cognoscenti were not sure,
Afraid of her bare-footed, flowing movements
Afraid before the terrible beauty of her red, Revolutionary dance
Afraid of her great, suffering soul.
She too, though white, was black and blue
Her bruises weeping through her art.

And I as well have wept, alone, at night, dancing to your
Terrible, searing songs, wept for all creation and men's wrongs
Wept for The Family, for Mississippi Goddamn, and wept that
             Everything Must Change.

The Hauntings

Rescued from the wreckage of the Past,
Memories cling, desperate for attention,
Wanting a home where they can settle
And fit in to a coherent pattern.

But they slide and slip,
Will not obey a structured form
And gradually become
A strange mosaic
Whose moving familiar unfamiliarity
Will not let me rest; but haunts me
Like a restless ghost
                searching for one who
Knew him and will offer him the
                recognition he so craves.

And I, who am too honest to
Pretend I know him well, will admit only
To remembrance of some parts or
Characteristics of the wraith, and

So the haunting story continues to unfold its
Strange and shifting path
Which I and my pursuing memories
                      must tread.

Tale Told in a Cab
to all the real London Cab Drivers

No, wait, wait, he said,
Looking at me fixedly in the driver's mirror
Traffic roaring round us – the Thames
A flash of haunting London –
Just listen. This 'ere cabbie picked 'im up, see,
Three years ago it was.
'Waterloo Station, Sir!' this geezer says –
A real City gent – but old-fashioned,
Bowler hat and rolled umbrella.

Where?, I said.
Got in at Bishopsgate
And when they got to Waterloo
He wasn't there!

But, I began ...

No, wait, wait, listen ...
He knew the geezer hadn't done a runner
So he asks the cabbie right behind
If he 'ad seen a gent get out.

No, was the reply – and there wasn't
No one *in* your cab.

God!, I said, it must have been ...

No, wait, wait, listen,
Some time later

This same cabbie picks up a
Fare at Bishopsgate, a woman,
And, suddenly, the City Gent was in the cab as well –
                    bowler hat and rolled umbrella –
And when the cabbie turns at Waterloo
To get his fare, he'd gone!
Did he get out? he asks the woman,
Who? she says

And then he knew

And for a while he never spoke of it
But then he learnt that other drivers
Had had the same experience of
Taking this poor ghost to Waterloo
And he had marvelled at it, unafraid,
                    honoured, perhaps.

And as I, too, alighted at the same sad station
That must house so many passing sorrows,
I mused upon the story;

          Who was he, what tormented
     Thoughts beneath that smooth and well turned-out
     Exterior of City Gent, seethed and
     Would not let him go, so that he still
     And still again would, with
     A nonchalant and ghostly flagging down
     With his so neatly rolled umbrella,
     Enter a cab and say, 'Waterloo Station, Sir!'?

The Power of Goodness

It was the man, a priest?, quietly standing there
In Parliament Square, holding up a cross,
That moved me to tears; traffic surging
Angrily across Westminster Bridge,
Newspaper headlines drumming out the crimes
Of fraudulent MPs, while mocking echoes
Of Wordsworth's simple sonnet
Whispered through the still damp print and
Demonstrating foreign agitators holding
Ominous black flags, massed threateningly,
Disregarding traffic, ambling tourists and police,
                    demanding to be heard.

        But, still, as I looked back
The priest was standing there, holding aloft
A rough wooden cross, quietly defying evil,
A prophet of Love and Goodness in the wilderness
                    of London, and the world,
                    and, overwhelmed, I wept.

The Breakthrough
or Vision of Arcadia

In the bank on a tearing suburban high street
Where litter and loud advertising
                    hold their own
The man before me in the queue,
Irregularly dressed, it's true,
No dull and slouching uniform
But a style that showed some
Individuality, broke
From this unromantic Century
And, proffering his cheque book,
Addressed the girl behind
The counter. 'Hello, rosy cheeks,'
He said, in pleasant tones of long ago

                    and suddenly

Birds sang,
          uncaring Time stopped wonderingly and
Gazed anew upon the lovely
Meadows flushing in the sun,
The glinting river,
The gentle breezes as they moved amongst the
Welcoming trees beneath whose bowering branches
Love-lorn shepherds
Sang their melodious songs to blushing maidens

While all the pure, enchanting intricacies
Of simple Nature
Rose
          and held the moment in eternity.

In the silent watches of the night

In the silent watches of the night
When the soul rises from her seeming slumbers
And, like a serious and truthful friend, tries to
Comfort you and still your anxious mind,
Take heed of the communion,
Listen to her reassurances, the silent wisdom
Of the soul; do not resist her peaceful mission,
Persisting in your common worrying,
But, gratefully and with a sense of joy,
Embrace her tender touch until you
Gradually throw off the lonely bonds of stress
And soar with her into those regions which
You know, you know are there
Waiting to welcome you into your rightful home.

My gentle Prince

My gentle prince from a far countree
Sings to me of sky and sea
Of grottos cool and forests deep
Where ancient Druids their watches keep.

He whispers, when I'm feeling low,
Of wondrous things and pathways bright
That lead beyond this dolorous place
To palaces of Truth and Grace.

He warms me when I'm feeling cold
And hums and murmurs tales of old,
Lying beside me on my bed
He tells me things that can't be said;

And often as I drift to sleep
I wonder at such Protean skill
That allows my gentle prince so wise
To assume a furry, feline guise.

Still Running

I've been on the run, now, for too long,
Resting only rarely
In odd shelters that seemed home
But the sea continually comes in with its near-death embrace
And, finally, choking, spews me up upon another
Barren jetty where the race continues,
Starting blocks and pistol causing me to stumble
So that I run on all fours for a time
                  staring at the surface of the earth.

And when I shakily stand up, still running,
Trying to even out my pace and catch my breath,
My dreams and nightmares rear up with me
While on the opposite bank gesticulating people roar, snatching at my soul,
                  Scylla and Charybdis closing in upon another victim.

And now, footsore and lacking in this barren time Odysseus's blessèd aid,
I limp and bleed and fade in hope,
Stiffen, find it difficult to turn my head to see my shadow;
                  but perhaps I am my shadow,
Perhaps those ever present monsters have succeeded
And this I thought myself is just my restless shadow, gliding, falling,
Caressing every angle and embrasure, suddenly rising,
Spreading, flying and then diving down beneath
My shadow feet, diminished into nothing,
                  a mere shadow of a shadow.

Yet still I'm running, trusting in the presence of my fluttering soul,
Looking for a shelter where the sea won't enter
Hoping for the gleam of Greece, the homecoming, the peace.

The Ship

This is the second time I've seen it
                    in my dreams
There in the cluttered house full of furniture and
                    clothes
                    old photographs
                    and memorabilia
The bright ribs of a ship.
New, curving wood
Shining
Like a strange skeleton waiting to be brought to life
Fleshed out into a magic vessel
And launched
          upon an unknown sea.

The Journey

In the Eighteen-Nineties they said it was built
But I knew it was made where there is no Time,
On the shores of Ancient Erin or Cornwall
Where horses galloped out of the foaming sea,
Tossing the spume from their manes, and
Calling their names loudly into the air which the elves
Then cunningly translated into 'Cupid' or 'David' or 'Joan'.
And, as lightning flashed over the sea and Thór
Strode the sky, the spell was cast
And the whirling carousel came into being;

        and was magicked
Into fairgrounds and fêtes where
Innocent people paid their money, climbed onto
The horses' backs, laughing and, for a while, carefree,
Thinking it a mere merry-go-round, there for their amusement.

        But had they looked
Into the horses' eyes, they would have known –
Those deep, unfathomable eyes which said,
'We still live in the ancient deeps
        still know the secrets
        of Poseidon and Athene – but the knowledge
Is not for you. Not yet. And so, being Time, for the time being,
We appear as wooden. Just listen to Grand Gavoli and
Watch his smiling master
        – and forget, forget!'

But then on Brockham Green, in
The middle of the Village Fair,
Poseidon with his retinue suddenly
Visited his wild and foaming horses;

Louder and louder played the expectant organ
And the smiling King of the Elves rang his magic bell,
Faster and faster sped the prancing steeds, pawing the pregnant air
And, as the sky, split by tongues of lightning,
                              deepened to darkness,
Thór crashed his mighty cymbals
And, casting spells of ice and runes of driving rain,
Poseidon, God of the Sea, arrived
            and the known and simple world
                              vanished.

But my prancing steed sped on through the darkness,
The little lights of the carousel glowing like beacons, while the
Elf-King rang his bell, smiling at me in his timeless wisdom,
And, sea-rain soaked, I heard the magic organ
Weaving its spell,
            faster and faster
                  and felt my horse flying
                        further and further

Until, suddenly, I was in another world
            faërie and flowing and full of music
                  and knew that, at last,
                        I had come home.

The Dissolving Divide

Yes, they exist, those places that the
Early Celtic Christians spoke of,
The 'thin places' where one seems to
Leave the earth and enter a divine dimension;
They exist;

It might be in a churchyard on a windy hill
                alone beside the moving sky,
Or the slow, dark green approach through ancient yews
To an old grey church upon an immemorial site,
Or the sudden unexpected clearing in the woods,
A forgotten trackway, or a stile beneath
A pondering oak, from which is glimpsed
Another world;
They exist, the thin places.

But do not seek them out,
Do not presume to find them,
For when the time is right
They will find you.

Suddenly, without warning,
You will be walking, out beyond this world,
Beyond the cares and petty tribulations
And you will be almost there
Where Reality exists in all its glory.

You will rise up as though on foamy clouds
To those heights seen in magic skies
When, as a child, all was mystery and wonder
When, radiantly oblivious to human limitation,
You ranged the vistas of imagination
And experienced the warm divinity of life.

You will be there with all the
Chorus of the heralding seers — the
                    Blackbird and the deer, the
                    Wonderful bee, the lion and
                    The ape, the crowing visionary cockerel.

You will be there — but only for a moment
And then the fall-back into everyday, wings lost.
But do not despair.
To once have been upon the threshold of Reality
Is reassurance, more would be too much to bear.

Be assured,
The glow of the experience is yours for ever
And common life will never be the same again.

The heartbeat of a bird

To enter into the life of things
Is to lose oneself
To flow out and into
        a leaf
        a bird

It is to leave one's body
        and become the leaf
And so it is that I often wonder
If I exist at all, so rarely do I feel at home
        inside this human form

So often do I feel the heartbeat of a bird.

The Garden Party

Oh yes, I was there at that illustrious party,
Inarticulate amongst such august hosts,
Circulating, glass in hand, but only able to
                              admire or smile,
Painfully aware I could not contribute to such a
                              great occasion,
An awed and silent guest witnessing
The magnificence and ritual;
The harmonious sounds of celebration
Bearing my senses to another sphere as I walked
Shyly through the colourful throng –

    Trembling delicate beauty side by side
    With sturdy masculine strength,
    Tentative débutantes and eager gleaming youths
    Watched by knowing chaperones,
    Brief flitting visitors from exotic climes,
    Workers still at work but pausing now and then
                       to celebrate;
    And then, suddenly, the joyous dancing and the games
    And all around such warmth and telling vibrancy
    One felt oneself to be upon the threshold of Reality.

Yes, I was there that rainy July dusk.
My faithful cat beside me,
Wandering amongst the beauty and the strength
Of trees, shrubs, birds, butterflies and bees and all the
Living world encompassed in that garden,
A wondering novice in the Realm of Truth and Beauty.

Late November Afternoon

So close to another dimension,
So thinly divided
                  and as the dusk
Sifts through the Autumn air
And trees stretch out their welcoming
Silhouettes, my soul grows luminous
With the sky, begins to fly
                          so close to home it hurts

                    and then it's dark
And yet another chance of entering Reality
Is lost,
Time reasserts its sway and carelessly
Continues on its bound and dreary way.

Melpomene

All whom she touches are affected.
Some never go back, but follow her through
Faërie regions and sad, weeping woods, alight with
The pure flame of Truth, Beauty and Compassion.
And even scholars, who on fewer whims are fed,
Wander, enchanted, in the Garden of her Verse;
Until they come upon a fountain cool
And two forking paths.
      Mostly, they return, by that which leads
Again to academe and peace; but those remaining,
As in a dream, walk on, along the way towards
The beckoning hazy sky and final freedom from
The World and all its clutching hands.

INDIA RUSSELL read German and Scandinavian at University College London and was appointed Junior Research Fellow in the Department of German at King's College, London. She holds a Speech and Drama Licentiate at Guildhall School of Music and Drama and trained in Contemporary Dance at The Place, performing with the Evening School Performance Group at The Place Theatre and the Lilian Baylis. She wrote and toured her own one-woman dance-drama on Ibsen's last plays, The Secret Rooms of the Mind. Her first collection of poetry, The Kaleidoscope of Time, went into its third impression in September, 2010.